**SCHIRMER'S LIBRARY OF MUSICAL CLASSICS**

Vol. 1766

SERGE PROKOFIEFF

Selected Works

For the Piano

Compiled by

ERNO BALOGH

ISBN 0-7935-5677-5

G. SCHIRMER, Inc.

DISTRIBUTED BY

7777 W. BLUEMOUND RD. P.O. BOX 13819 MILWAUKEE, WI 53213

CONTENTS

Etude, Op. 2, No. 3

Serge Prokofieff,
(1909)

Piano

Presto

ritardando

dim.

p cresc.

cresc. | *e accelerando*

Prestissimo

A Monsieur Alexandre Winkler

Etude in C minor

Specially edited by
the Composer

Serge Prokofieff, Op. 2, No. 4
(1909)

Presto energico (♩ = 152)

Conte

Serge Prokofieff, Op. 3, No. 1
(1907-11)

Badinage

Serge Prokofieff, Op. 3, No. 2
(1907-11)

Marche

Serge Prokofieff, Op. 3, No. 3
(1908)

Allegro energico

Fantôme

Serge Prokofieff, Op. 3, No. 4
(1907)

Presto tenebroso

pp sempre una corda

Suggestion Diabolique

Serge Prokofieff, Op. 4, No. 4
(1908-11)

Prestissimo fantastico

42932

Toccata

Serge Prokofieff, Op. 11
(1912)

Allegro marcato

42932

à M. Basile Moroleff

March in F minor

Specially edited by
The Composer

Serge Prokofieff, Op. 12, No. 1
(1906-13)

Prélude

Specially edited by
the Composer

Serge Prokofieff, Op. 12, No. 7
(1913)

42932

Gavotte

from the "Classical Symphony"

Serge Prokofieff, Op. 25
(1916-17)
Arranged by the Composer

Non troppo allegro

March
from "The Love of Three Oranges"

Serge Prokofieff, Op. 33
(1919)
Arranged by the Composer

Tempo di Marcia

Chose en soi

Serge Prokofieff, Op. 45b
(1928)

Andante sostenuto

à Vladimir Horowitz

Scherzo

Serge Prokofieff, Op. 52, No. 6
(1909-31)

Sonatina in G major

I

Serge Prokofieff, Op. 54, No. 2
(1932)

Allegro sostenuto (♩ = 104–108)

42932

II

Andante amabile (♩ = 76)

III

Allegro, ma non troppo (♩ = 168)

82

Tempo primo

Paysage

Serge Prokofieff, Op. 59, No. 2
(1933)

à Nicolas Orloff

Scherzino

Serge Prokofieff, Op. 52, No. 4
(1920-31)

Sonatine Pastorale in C major

Serge Prokofieff, Op. 59, No. 3
(1934)

96

42932

Più mosso (Tempo iniziale)

Poco più animato

Pensées

Serge Prokofieff, Op. 62, No.1
(1933-34)

I

Pensées

II

Serge Prokofieff, Op. 62, No. 2
(1933-34)

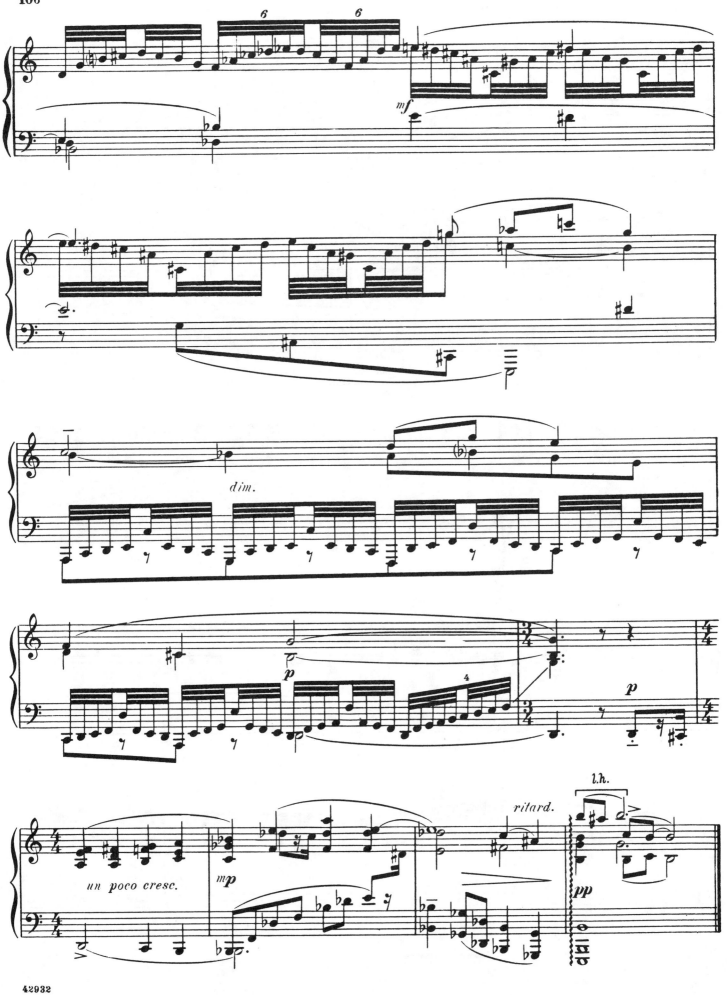

Pensées

Serge Prokofieff, Op. 62, No. 3
(1933 - 34)

III

Gavotte

Serge Prokofieff, Op. 77, No. 4
(1938)

Contradance

from the film "Lermontov"

Serge Prokofieff, Op. 96, No. 2
(1943)

Mephisto Valse

from the film "Lermontov"

Serge Prokofieff, Op. 96, No. 3
(1943)

42932

Allegro precipitato, come prima